HAL LEONARD

EASY BANJO SOLOS

BY MAC ROBERTSON

Welcome to *Easy Banjo Solos*, a collection of 16 timeless songs arranged for 5-string banjo. This beginner's songbook can be used on its own or as a supplement to the *Hal Leonard Banjo Method*, or any other beginning banjo method. The songs are arranged in order of difficulty and presented in an easy-to-follow format, with the melody line on the top staff and the banjo solo on the bottom staff.

Every song in the book includes a full audio demo track of the banjo arrangement with banjo accompaniment. The first two tracks also feature slow demos to help you get started. Use the audio demo tracks online, for download or streaming!

To access audio visit:
www.halleonard.com/mylibrary
Enter Code
4450-2103-8619-6822

The author gratefully acknowledges Jon Peik's assistance with arrangements and accompaniment.
Recording credits: Mac Robertson – banjo, bass, and guitar; Jon Peik – guitar and banjo

ISBN 978-1-4803-0921-0

HAL•LEONARD®
CORPORATION

7777 W. BLUEMOUND RD. P.O. BOX 13819 MILWAUKEE, WI 53213

Visit Hal Leonard Online at
www.halleonard.com

TOM DOOLEY

Words and Music Collected, Adapted and Arranged by
Frank Warner, John A. Lomax and Alan Lomax
From the singing of Frank Proffitt

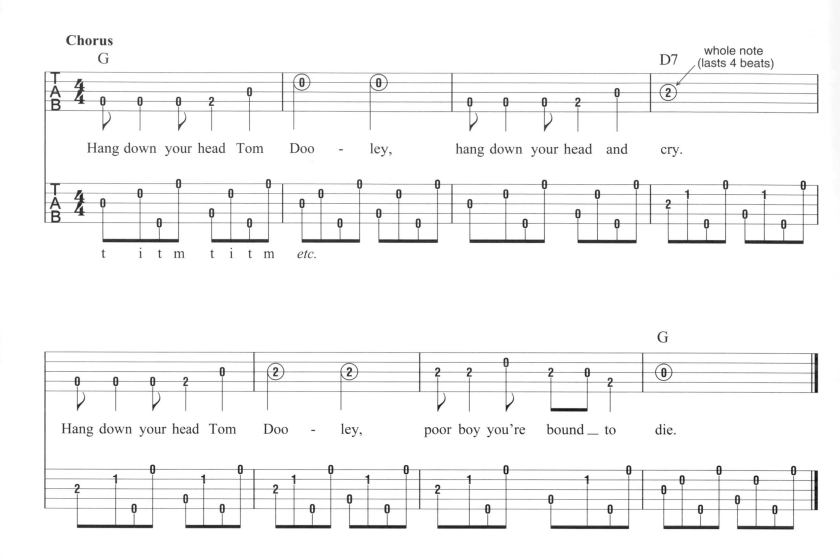

Additional Verses

1. Met her on the mountain,
   Said she'd be my wife,
   But the gal refused me,
   Stabbed her with my knife. *CHORUS*

2. 'Bout this time tomorrow
   Reckon where I'll be,
   Down in some lonesome valley
   Hanging from a big oak tree. *CHORUS*

ROCKY TOP

Words and Music by Boudleaux Bryant
and Felice Bryant

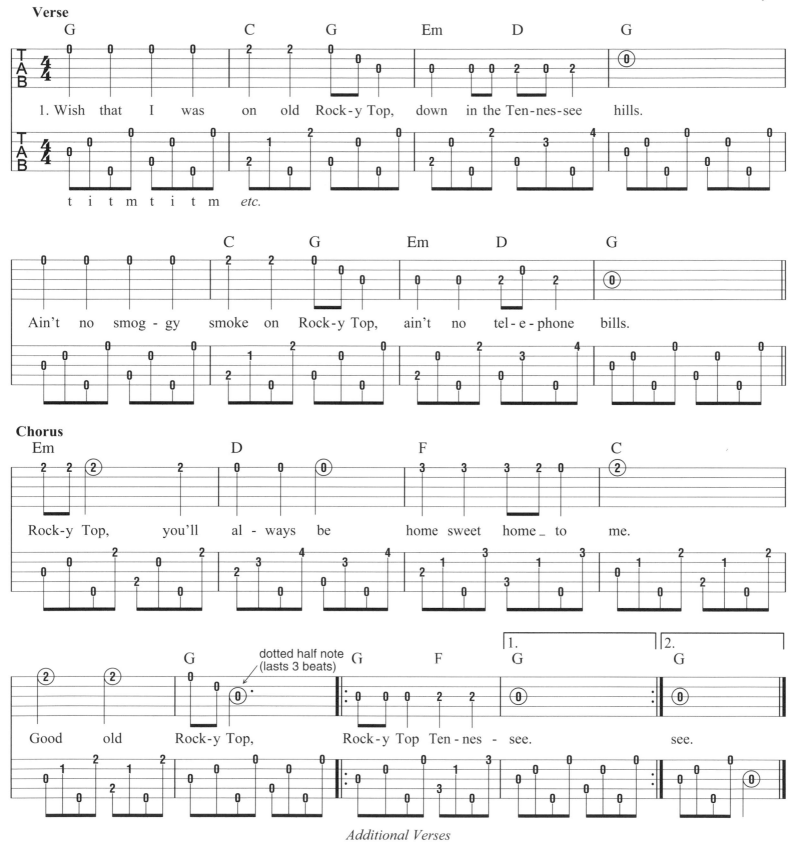

Additional Verses

2. Once two strangers climbed ol' Rocky Top lookin' for a moonshine still.
   Strangers ain't come down from Rocky Top; reckon they never will. *CHORUS*

3. Corn won't grow at all on Rocky Top; dirt's too rocky by far.
   That's why all the folks on Rocky Top get their corn from a jar. *CHORUS*

THIS LAND IS YOUR LAND

Words and Music by
Woody Guthrie

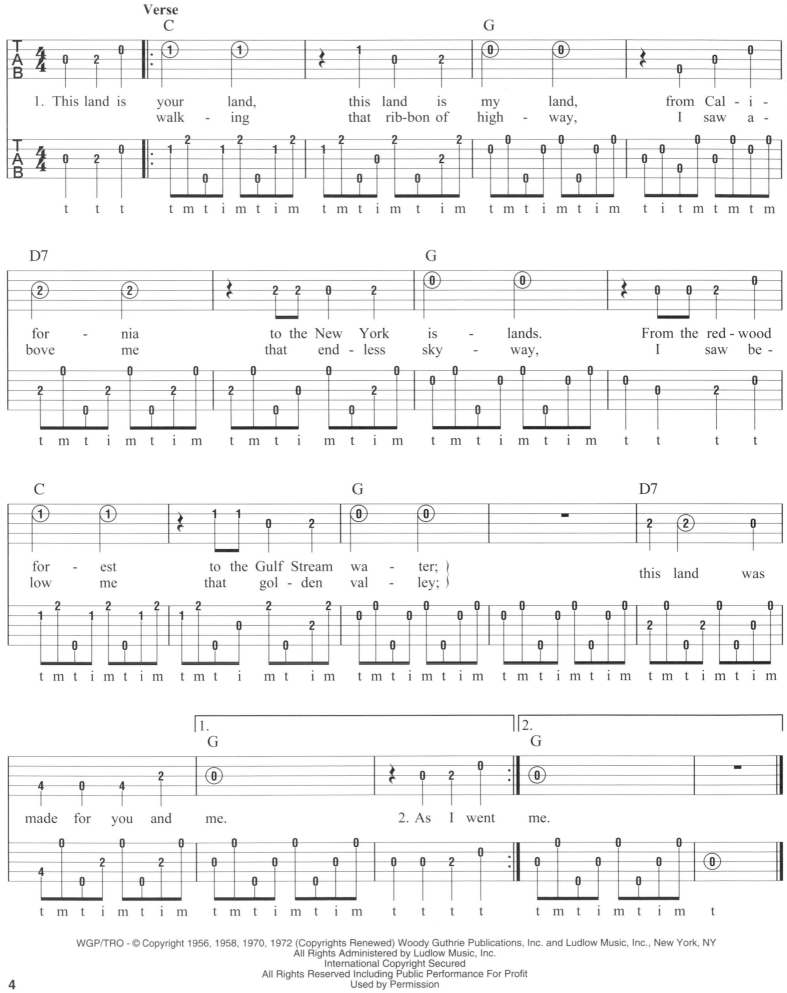

WABASH CANNONBALL

Words and Music by
A.P. Carter

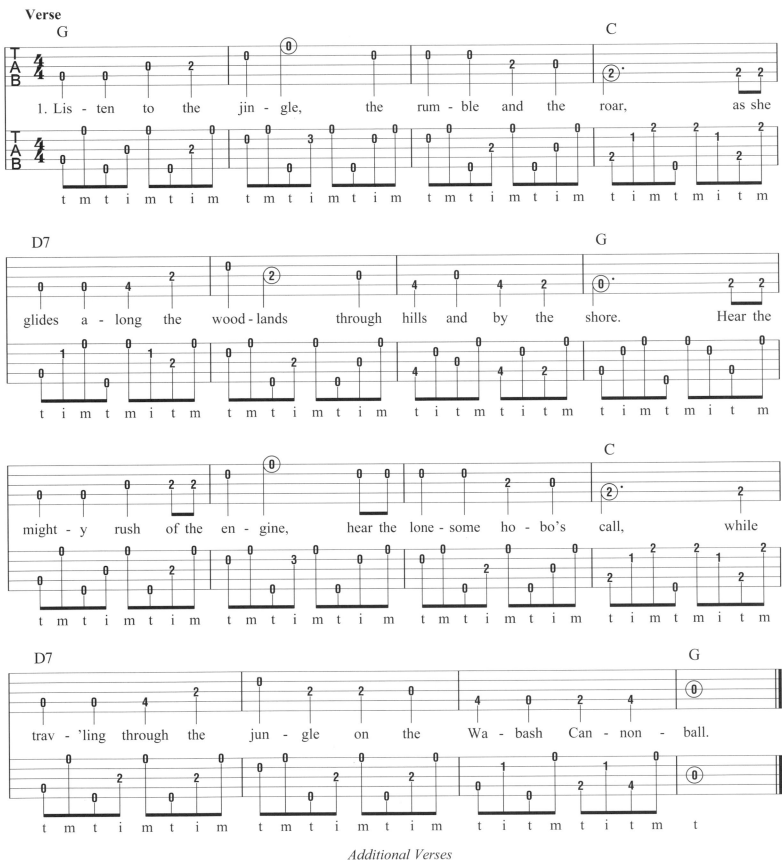

Additional Verses

2. Now the eastern states are dandy, so the western people say,
   From New York to St. Louis and Chicago by the way.
   From the hills of Minnesota where the rippling waters fall,
   No changes can be taken on the Wabash Cannonball.

OH, LONESOME ME

Words and Music by
Don Gibson

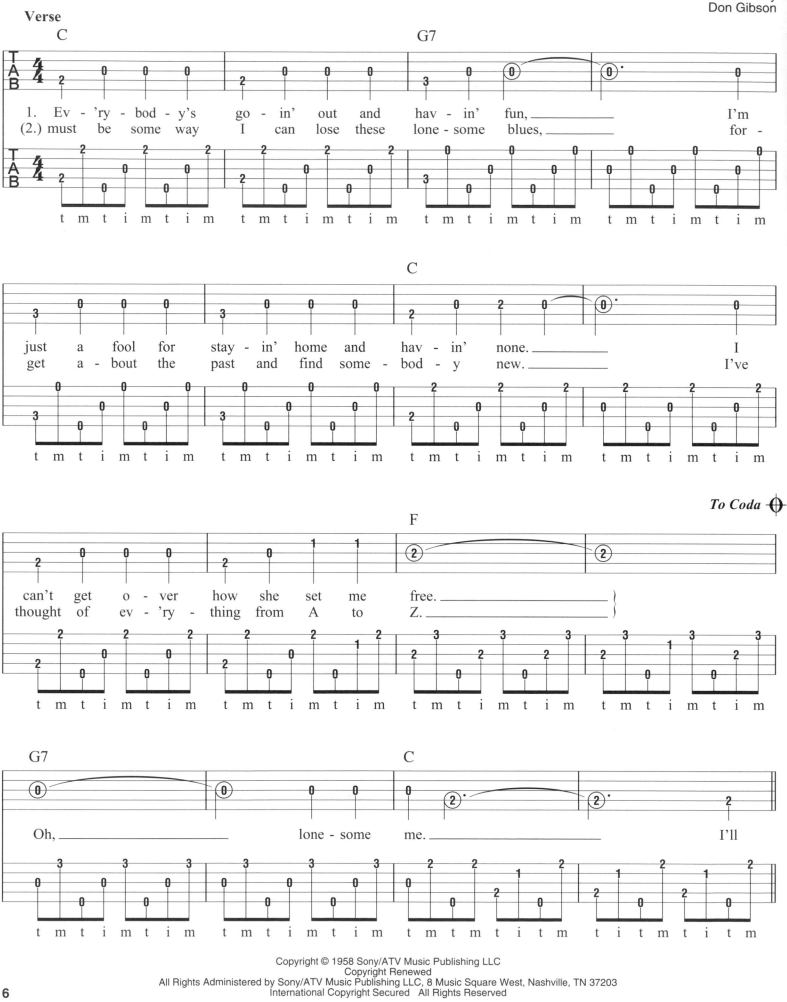

Bridge

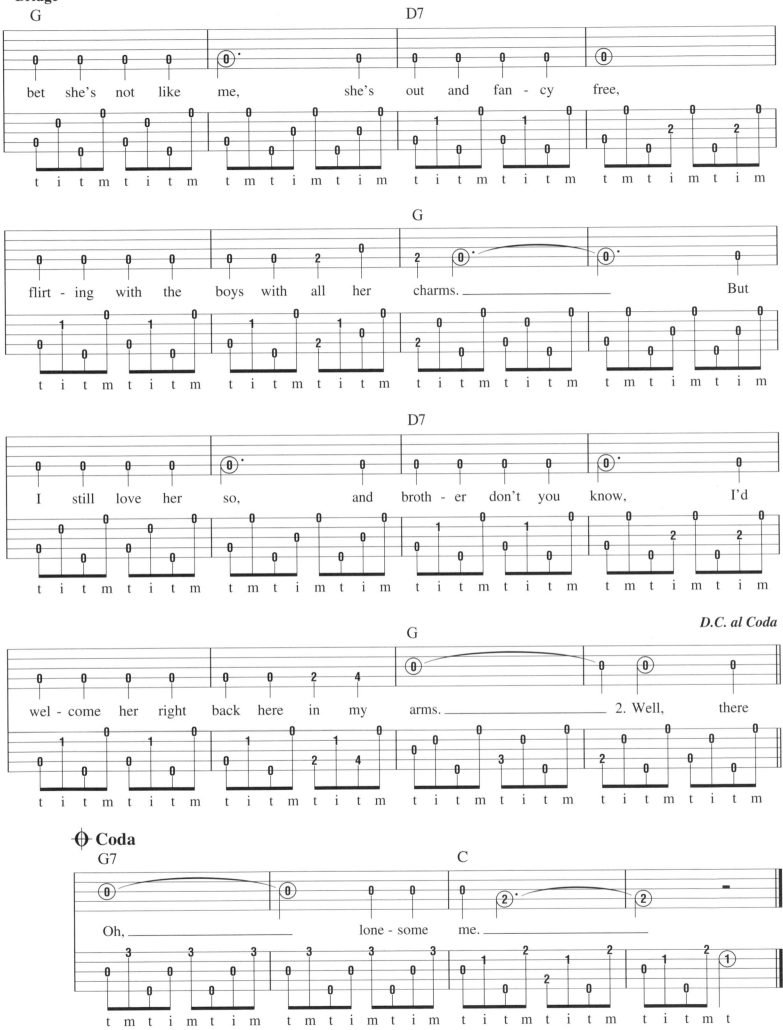

I'VE JUST SEEN A FACE

Words and Music by John Lennon
and Paul McCartney

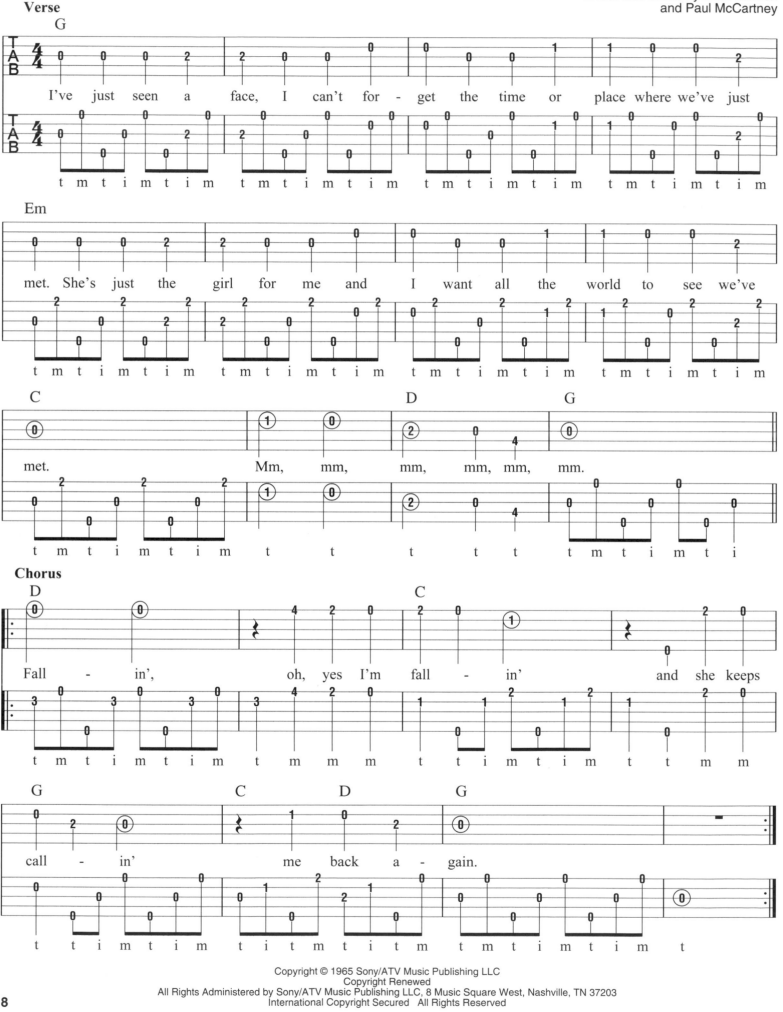

WILL THE CIRCLE BE UNBROKEN

Words by Ada R. Habershon
Music by Charles H. Gabriel

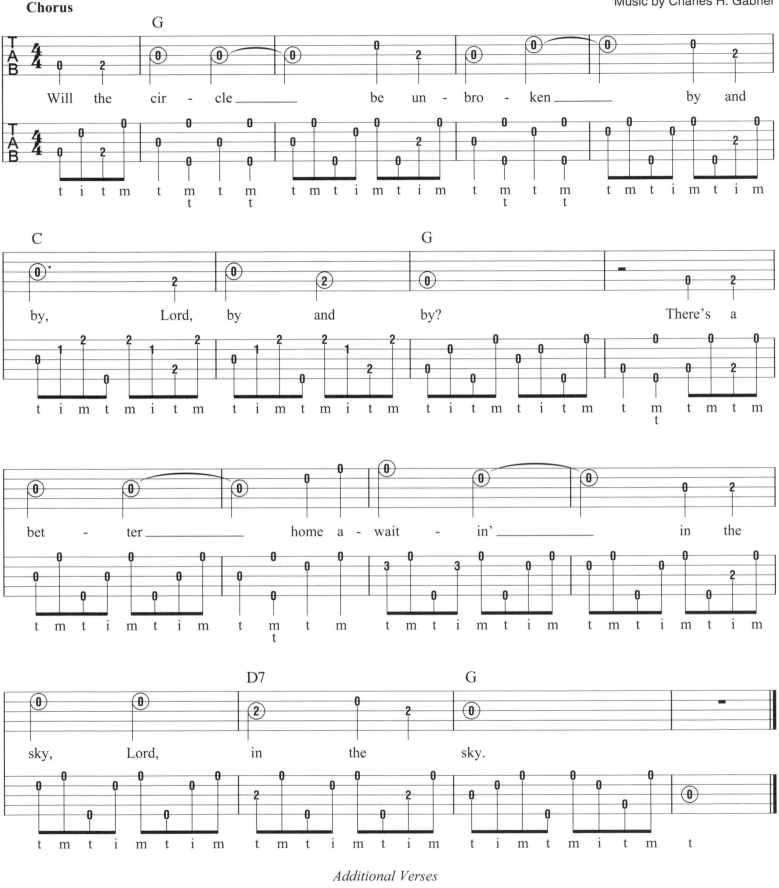

Additional Verses

1. I was standing by my window
   On a cold and cloudy day,
   When I saw that hearse come rolling
   For to carry my mother away. *CHORUS*

2. Lord, I told that undertaker
   Undertaker please drive slow,
   For this body that you're hauling
   Lord, I hate to see her go. *CHORUS*

3. I followed close behind her
   Tried to hold up and be brave,
   But I could not hide my sorrow
   When they laid her in the grave. *CHORUS*

BALLAD OF JED CLAMPETT

from the Television Series THE BEVERLY HILLBILLIES

Words and Music by Paul Henning

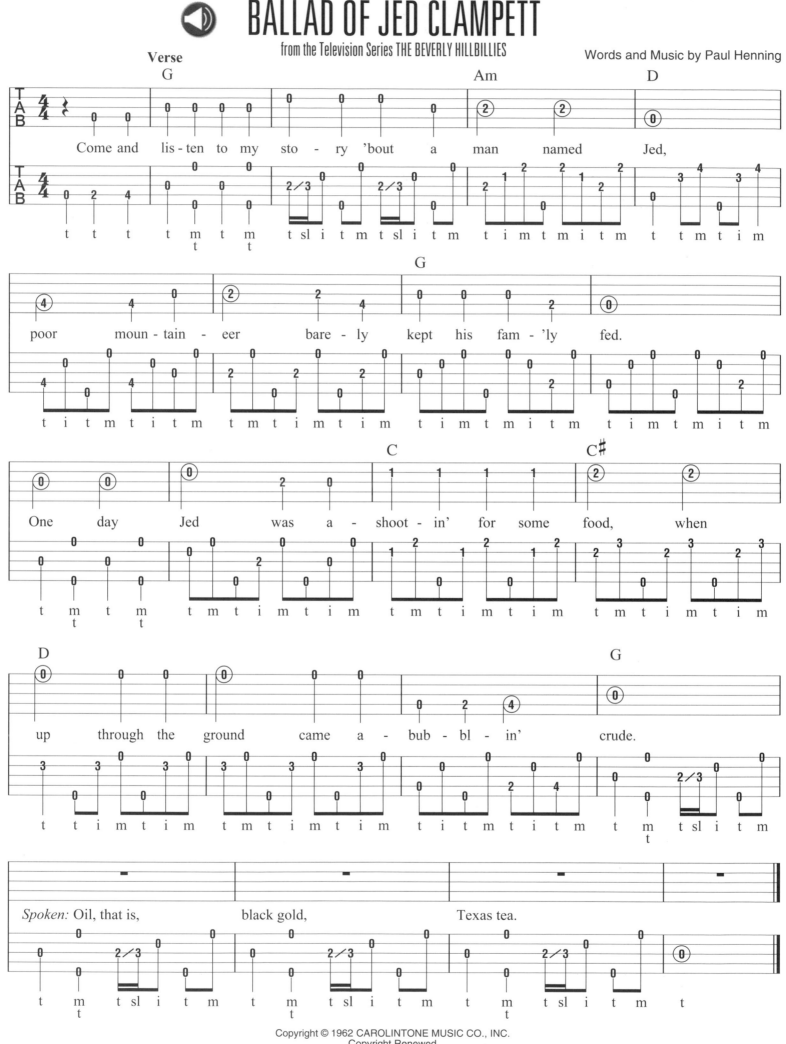

MOUNTAIN DEW

Words and Music by Scott Wiseman
and Bascomb Lunsford

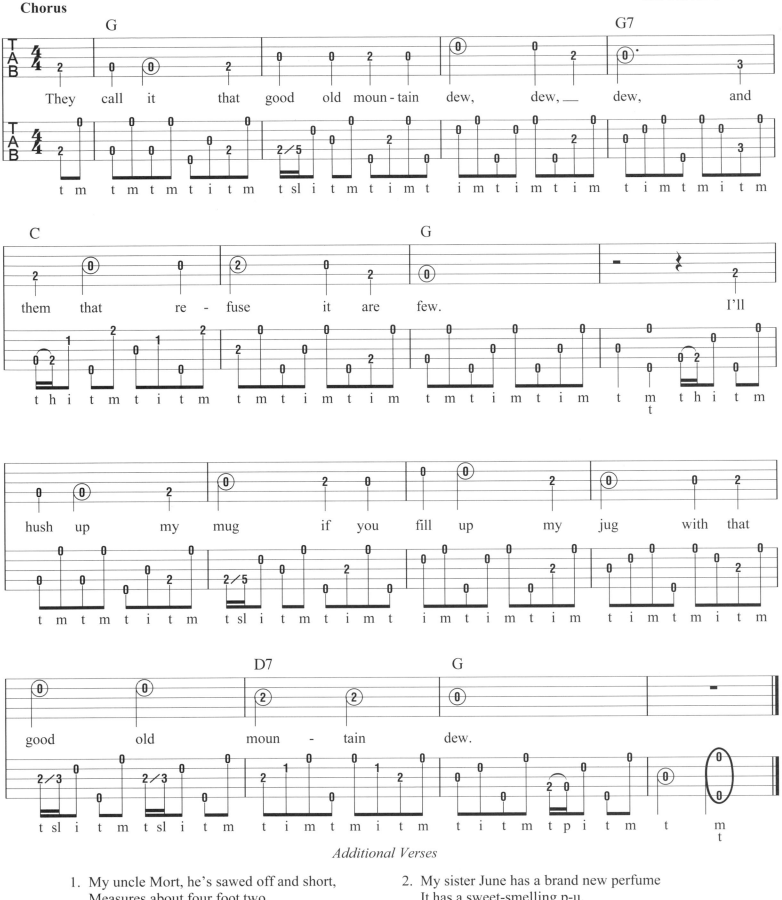

Additional Verses

1. My uncle Mort, he's sawed off and short,
   Measures about four foot two,
   But he thinks he's a giant if you give him a pint,
   Of that good old mountain dew.

2. My sister June has a brand new perfume
   It has a sweet-smelling p-u.
   Imagine her surprise when she had it analyzed,
   'Twas nothin' but good old mountain dew.

I'LL FLY AWAY

Words and Music by
Albert E. Brumley

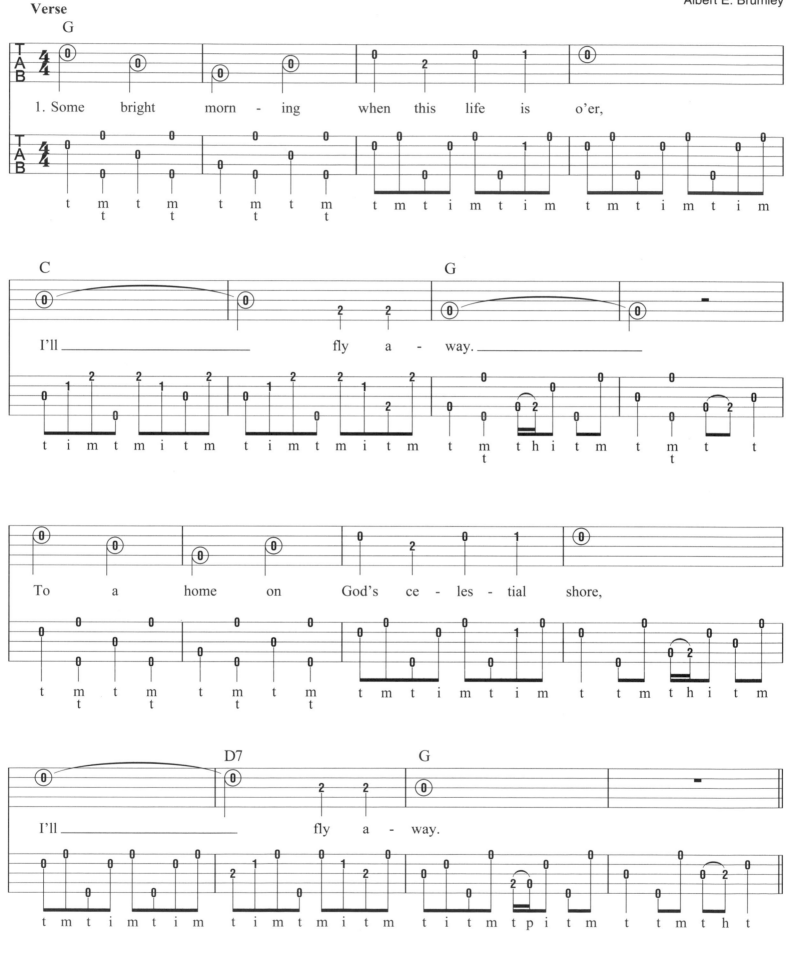

Chorus

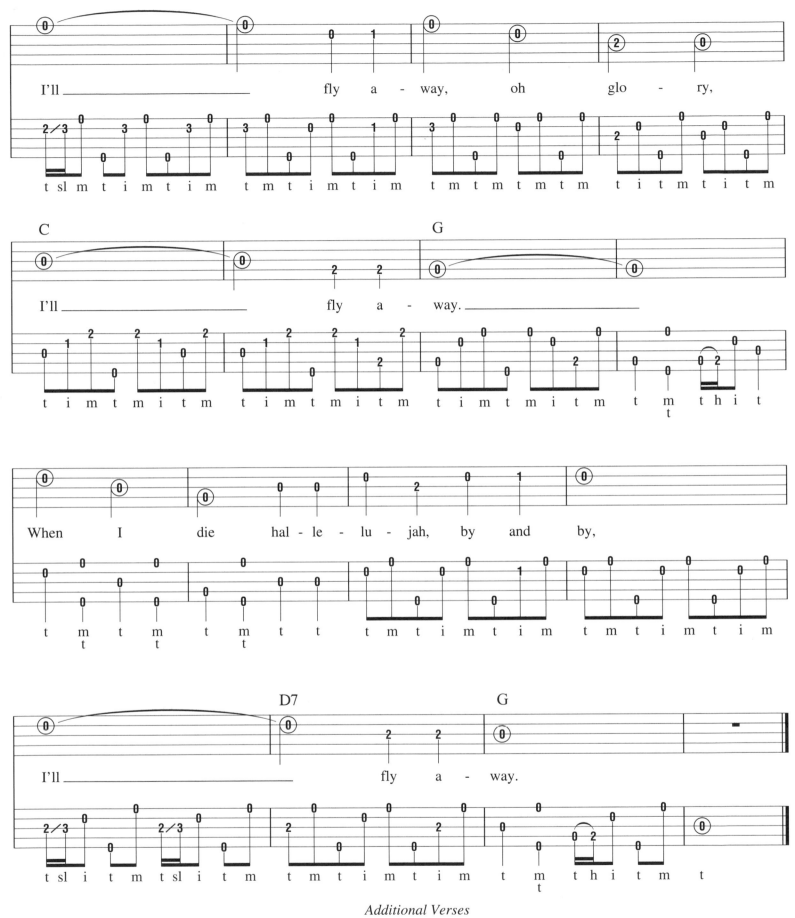

Additional Verses

1. When the shadows of this life have grown, I'll fly away.
   Like a bird that from prison bars has flown, I'll fly away. *CHORUS*

2. Just a few more weary days and then, I'll fly away.
   To a land where joy shall never end, I'll fly away. *CHORUS*

WAGON WHEEL

Words and Music by Ketch Secor
and Bob Dylan

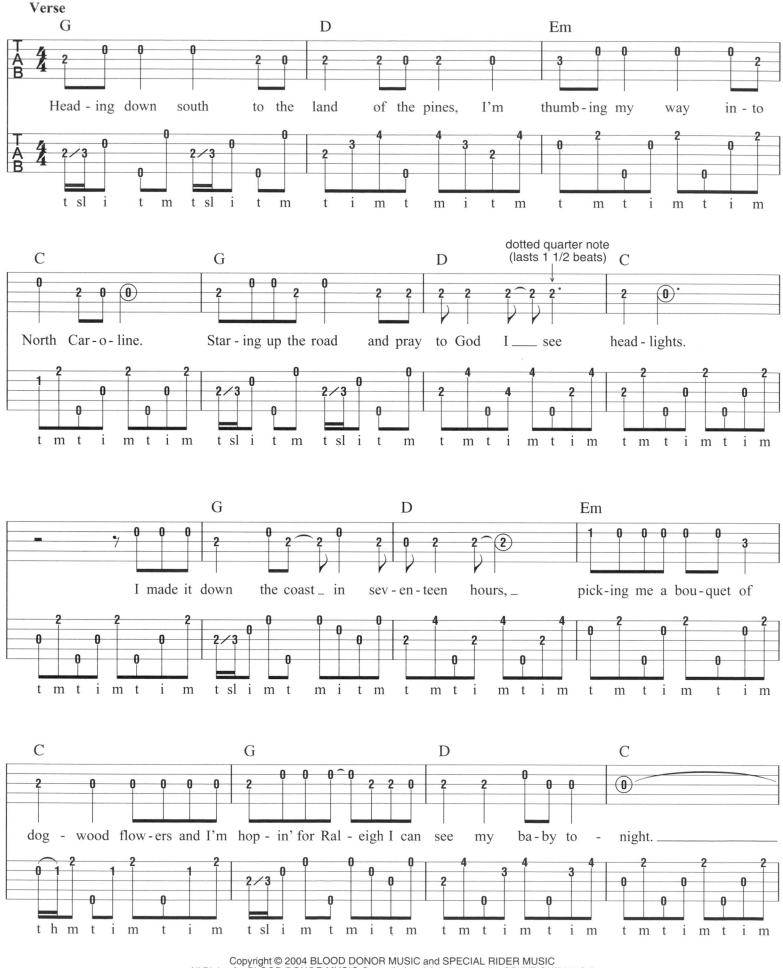

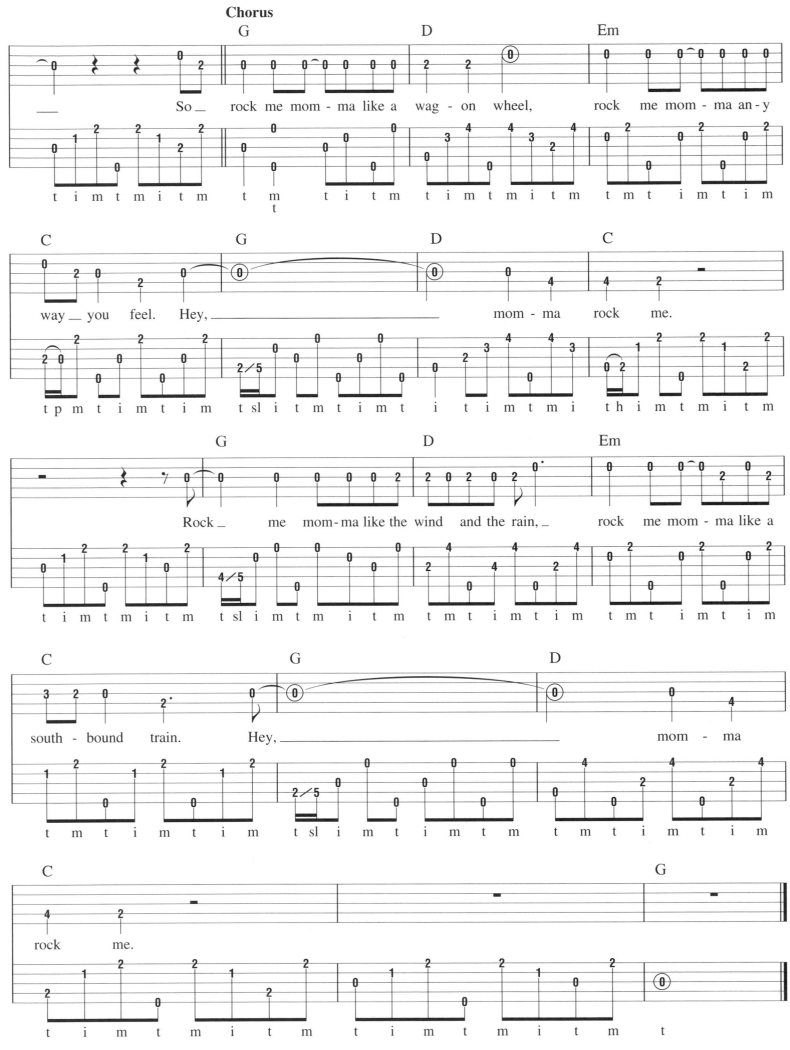

ASHOKAN FAREWELL
Theme from PBS Series THE CIVIL WAR

By Jay Ungar

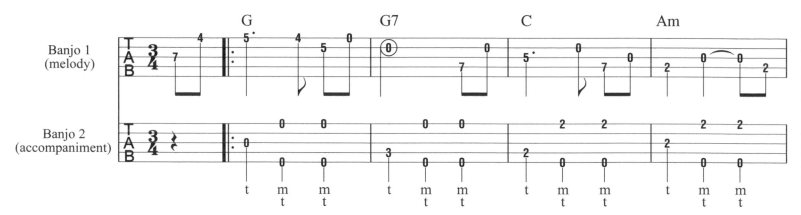

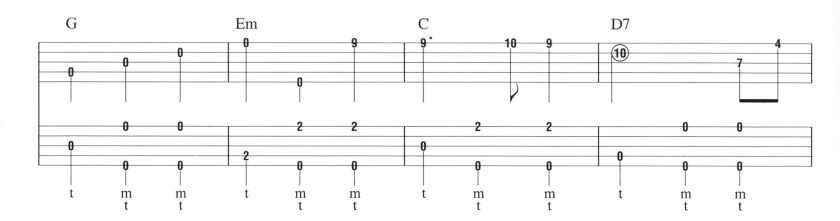

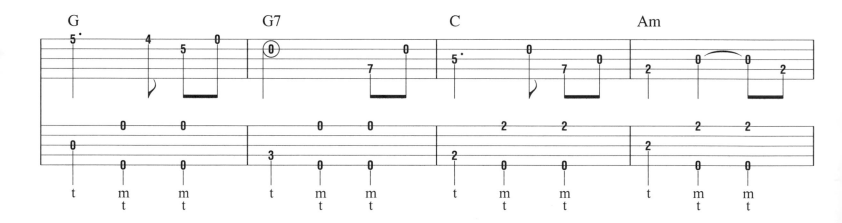

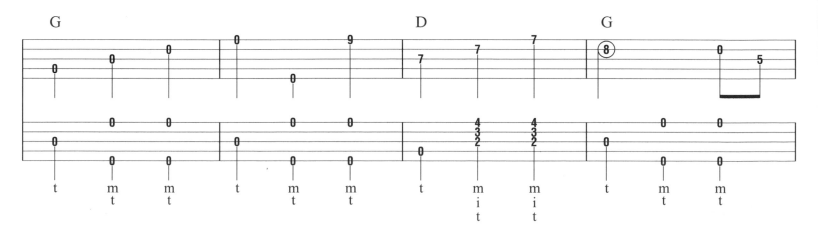

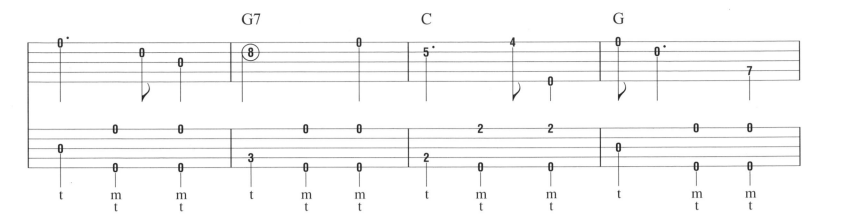

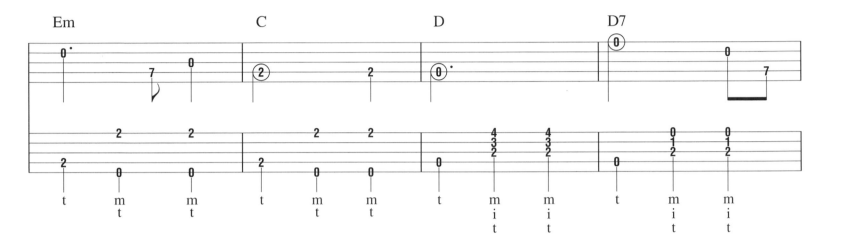

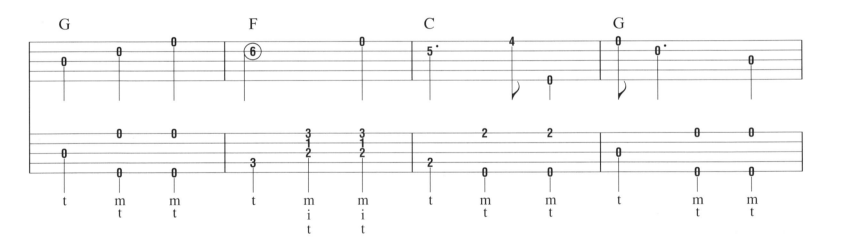

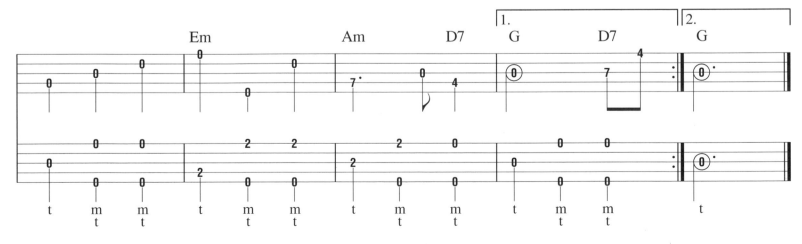

I SAW THE LIGHT

Words and Music by
Hank Williams

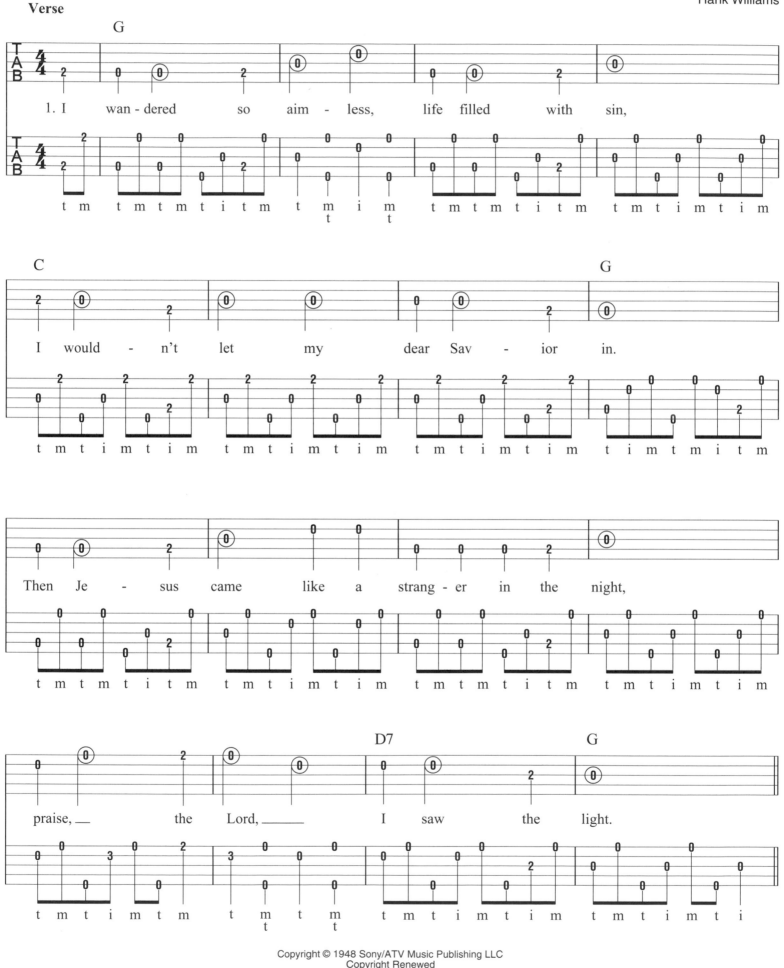

Chorus

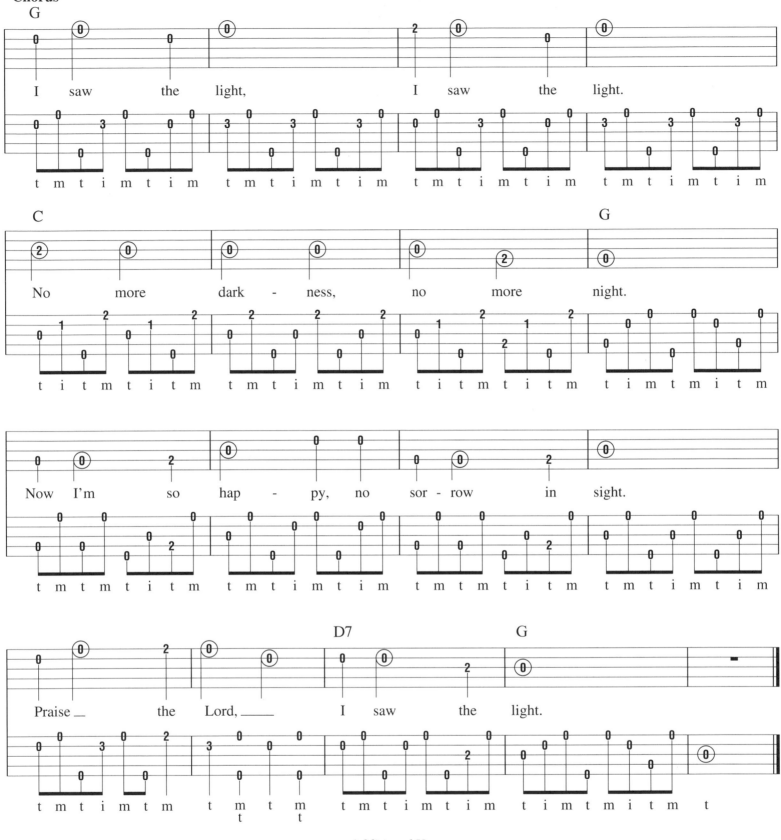

Additional Verses

2. Just like a blind man, I wandered alone.
   Worries and fears I claimed for my own.
   Then like the blind man that God gave back his sight,
   Praise the Lord, I saw the light. *CHORUS*

3. I was a fool to wander and stray.
   Straight is the gate and narrow the way.
   Now I have traded the wrong for the right,
   Praise the Lord, I saw the light. *CHORUS*

HEY, GOOD LOOKIN'

Words and Music by
Hank Williams

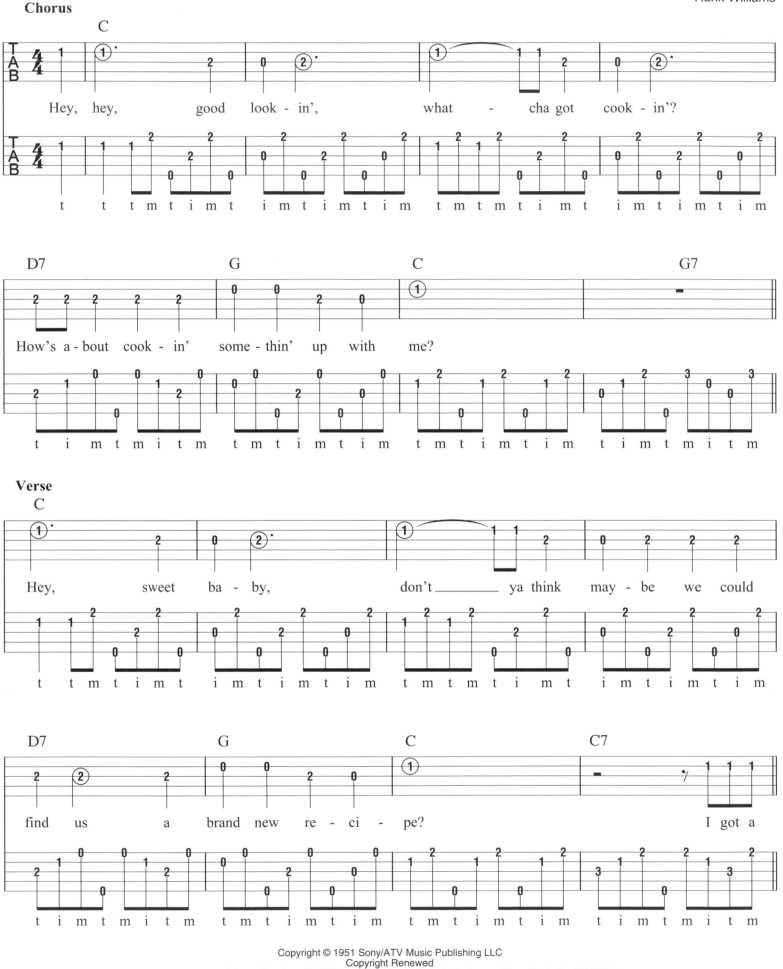

Bridge

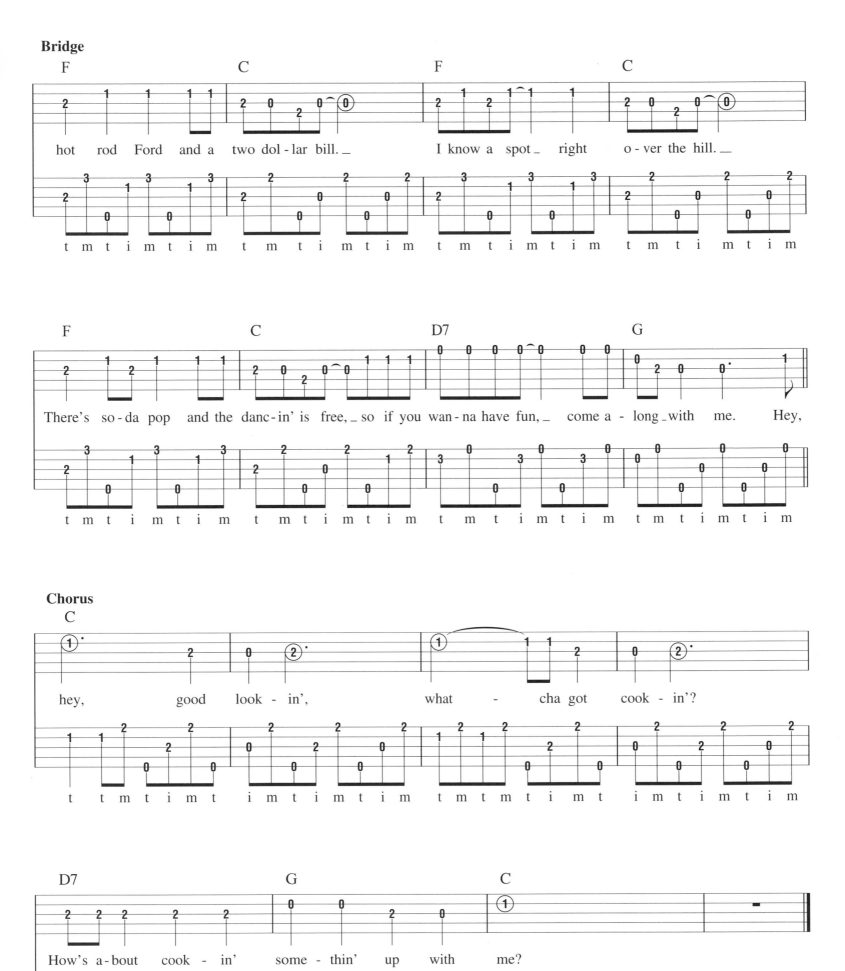

Chorus

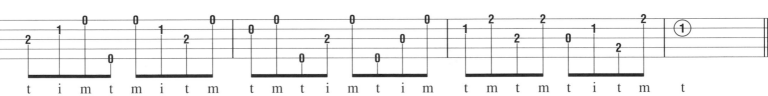

BLACK DIAMOND

Words and Music by
Don Stover

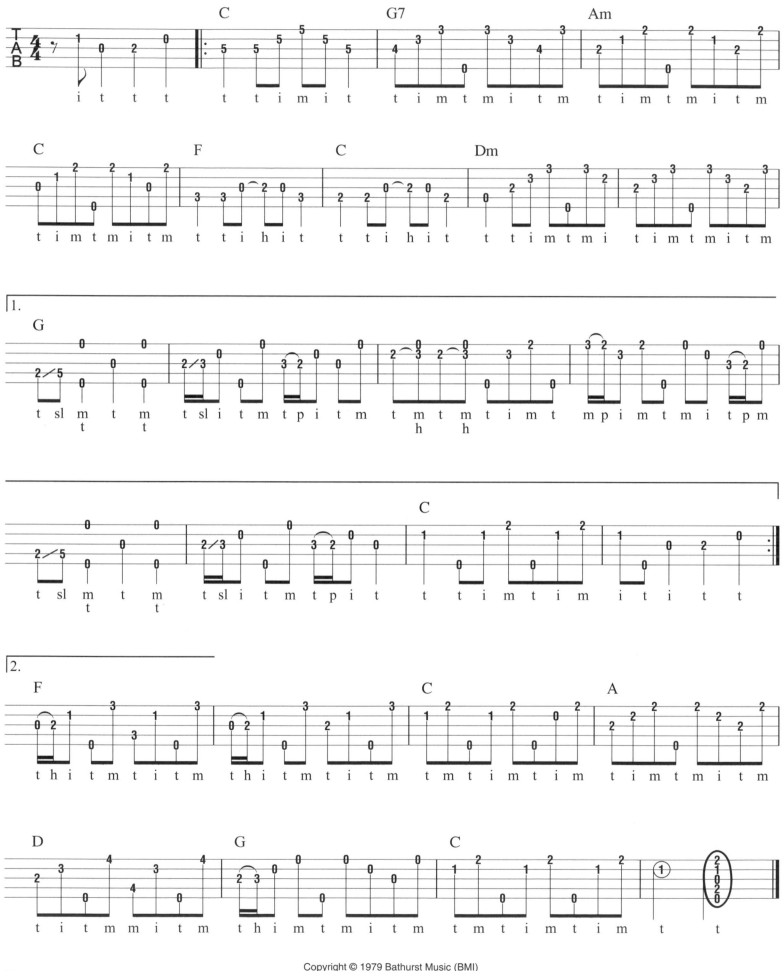

NINE POUND HAMMER

Words and Music by
Merle Travis

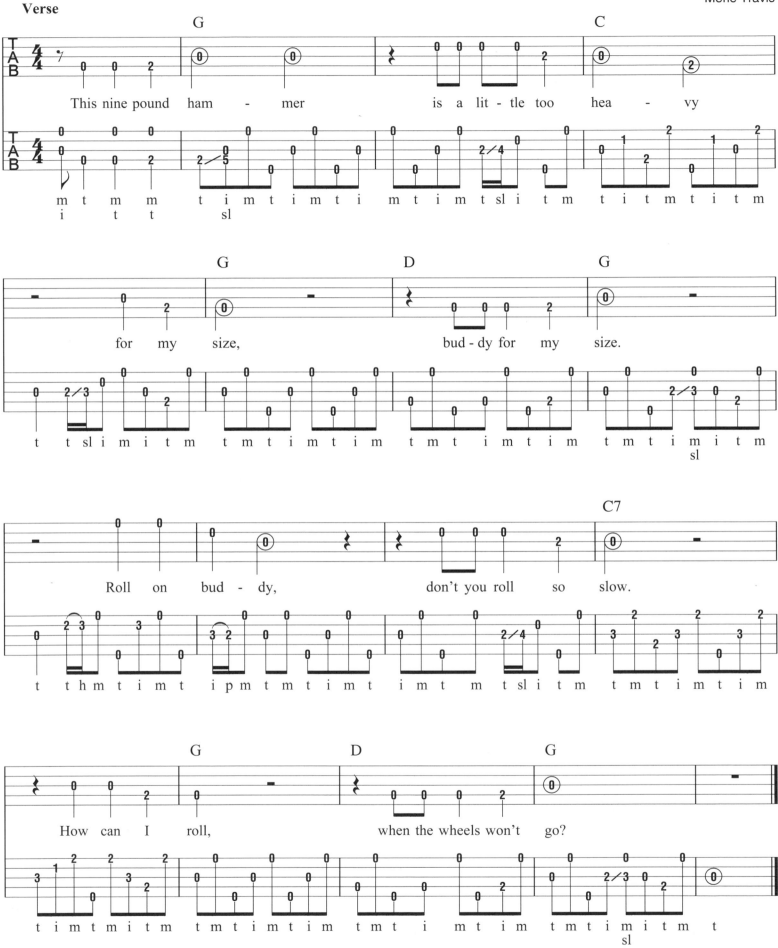

GREAT BANJO PUBLICATIONS

FROM HAL LEONARD CORPORATION

Hal Leonard Banjo Method – Second Edition

by Mac Robertson, Robbie Clement, Will Schmid
This innovative method teaches 5-string banjo blue-grass style using a carefully paced approach that keeps beginners playing great songs *while learning*. Book 1 covers easy chord strums, tablature, right-hand rolls, hammer-ons, slides and pull-offs, and more. Book 2 includes solos and licks, fiddle tunes, back-up, capo use, and more.

00699500	Book 1 (Book Only)	$7.99
00695101	Book 1 (Book/CD Pack)	$16.99
00699502	Book 2 (Book Only)	$7.99

Banjo Chord Finder

This extensive reference guide covers over 2,800 banjo chords, including four of the most commonly used tunings. Thirty different chord qualities are covered for each key, and each chord quality is presented in two different voicings. Also includes a lesson on chord construction and a fingerboard chart of the banjo neck!

00695741	9 x 12	$6.99
00695742	6 x 9	$5.95

Banjo Scale Finder

by Chad Johnson
Learn to play scales on the banjo with this comprehensive yet easy-to-use book. It contains more than 1,300 scale diagrams for the most often-used scales and modes, including multiple patterns for each scale. Also includes a lesson on scale construction and a fingerboard chart of the banjo neck.

00695780	9 x 12	$6.95
00695783	6 x 9	$5.95

The Beatles for Banjo

18 of the Fab Four's finest for five string banjo! Includes: Across the Universe • Blackbird • A Hard Day's Night • Here Comes the Sun • Hey Jude • Let It Be • She Loves You • Strawberry Fields Forever • Ticket to Ride • Yesterday • and more.

00700813 ....$14.99

Christmas Favorites for Banjo

27 holiday classics arranged for banjo, including: Blue Christmas • Feliz Navidad • Frosty the Snow Man • Grandma's Killer Fruitcake • A Holly Jolly Christmas • I Saw Mommy Kissing Santa Claus • It's Beginning to Look like Christmas • Jingle-Bell Rock • Nuttin' for Christmas • Rudolph the Red-Nosed Reindeer • Silver Bells • and more.

00699109..$10.95

Fretboard Roadmaps

by Fred Sokolow
This handy book/CD pack will get you playing all over the banjo fretboard in any key! You'll learn to: increase your chord, scale and lick vocabulary • play chord-based licks, moveable major and blues scales, melodic scales and first-position major scales • and much more! The CD includes 51 demonstrations of the exercises.

00695358 Book/CD Pack $14.95

O Brother, Where Art Thou?

Banjo tab arrangements of 12 bluegrass/folk songs from this Grammy-winning album. Includes: The Big Rock Candy Mountain • Down to the River to Pray • I Am a Man of Constant Sorrow • I Am Weary (Let Me Rest) • I'll Fly Away • In the Jailhouse Now • Keep on the Sunny Side • You Are My Sunshine • and more, plus lyrics and a banjo notation legend.

00699528 Banjo Tablature.......................... $12.95

Earl Scruggs and the 5-String Banjo

Earl Scruggs' legendary method has helped thousands of banjo players get their start. It features everything you need to know to start playing, even how to build your own banjo! Topics covered include: Scruggs tuners • how to read music • chords • how to read tablature • anatomy of Scruggs-style picking • exercises in picking • 44 songs • biographical notes • and more! The CD features Earl Scruggs playing and explaining over 60 examples!

00695764	Book Only	$19.95
00695765	Book/CD Pack	$34.99

The Tony Trischka Collection

59 authentic transcriptions by Tony Trischka, one of the world's best banjo pickers and instructors. Includes: Blown Down Wall • China Grove • Crossville Breakdown • Heartlands • Hill Country • Kentucky Bullfight • A Robot Plane Flies over Arkansas • and more. Features an introduction by Béla Fleck, plus Tony's comments on each song. Transcriptions are in tab only.

00699063 Banjo Tablature.......................... $19.95

The Ultimate Banjo Songbook

A great collection of banjo classics: Alabama Jubilee • Bye Bye Love • Duelin' Banjos • The Entertainer • Foggy Mountain Breakdown • Great Balls of Fire • Lady of Spain • Orange Blossom Special • (Ghost) Riders in the Sky • Rocky Top • San Antonio Rose • Tennessee Waltz • UFO-TOFU • You Are My Sunshine • and more.

00699565 Book/2-CD Pack $24.95

FOR MORE INFORMATION, SEE YOUR LOCAL MUSIC DEALER,
OR WRITE TO:

7777 W. BLUEMOUND RD. P.O. BOX 13819 MILWAUKEE, WI 53213

Prices, contents, and availability subject to change without notice.

Visit Hal Leonard online at **www.halleonard.com**

0514